HIGH-PERFORMANCE TEAMS:
THE FOUNDATIONS

Richard Kasperowski

High-Performance Teams: The Foundations

Published by C4Media, publisher of InfoQ.com.

ISBN: 978-0-359-19418-6

Production Editor: Ana Ciobotaru
Copy Editor: Lawrence Nyveen
Design: Dragos Balasoiu

Contents

PART
ONE

Introduction

Back in 1990 in *Flow: The Psychology of Optimal Experience*,[1] Mihaily Csíkszentmihályi put forward the theory that people are happiest when in a state of flow — a condition of being totally absorbed and focused on the activity they're involved in, to the point that nothing else seems to matter. When this happens at work, you're completely on top of your game — productive, engaged, and absolutely fulfilled. It's a state of intrinsic motivation, in which you feel great and the results speak for themselves.

When a team is in flow is when the magic really happens.

Not only do people love the work they're doing, their enthusiasm and effectiveness create a positive feedback loop, and they become greater than the sum of their parts. Performance and output are optimized, and the experience is too.

When you find yourself part of a team like this, it can feel like the greatest good fortune — a fragile coincidence of task, personality, and some unknown alignment of the stars that feels almost counterproductive to examine too closely. After all, while you're all in the zone, you'd better just roll with it and get stuff done!

But the truth is it's not coincidence. High-performing teams don't happen by chance: certain factors directly contribute (or not) to this outcome. The evidence is in; there's data on what works. And the good news is there are protocols and behaviors that any team leader can introduce — in any team — that will improve the effectiveness of how you all communicate and work together.

This ebook will help you get started.

---

1   http://www.pursuit-of-happiness.org/history-of-happiness/mihaly-csikszentmihalyi/

About Richard Kasperowski

Richard Kasperowski is a speaker, teacher, coach, and author focused on high-performance teams. Kasperowski is the author of The Core Protocols: A Guide to Greatness. He leads clients in building great teams that get great results using the Core Protocols,  agile, and open-space technology. Richard created and teaches the course Agile Software Development at Harvard University.

To learn more visit kasperowski.com

About the Core Protocols

This guide draws extensively upon the work of Jim and Michele McCarthy in *The Core Protocols* — they did the original research on effective behaviors for team performance at McCarthy Technologies, Inc. It was their observations and testing with hundreds of groups of people that led them to distill the essence of team greatness into the deceptively simple open-source protocols that form the basic operational guide for success — the foundation of all the work which others and I have done since in this space.

For easy reference, I have included the Core Protocols in full in the appendix.

PART TWO

Underpinning everything with positivity

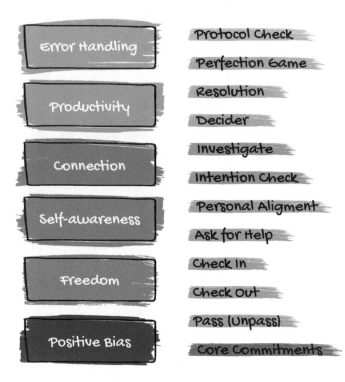

Think about the times you have done your greatest work. Can you produce your best results if you're not in an open and positive frame of mind? It's the same when you're working together in a team. Openness keeps you flexible and able to see potential and synergistic solutions rather than fixating on problems and getting stuck. It helps you develop a growth mindset where abundance comes naturally, rather than the zero-sum economics of scarcity and a fixed outlook.

There is a profound connection between greatness and happiness, between high performance and love. Positivity feeds itself and grows, inspiring greater levels of satisfaction and accomplishment, in a high-gain loop. Achieving the effortlessness of a flow state is greatly facilitated by a bias to optimism and action, a conscious choice to opt for growth rather than decline, for abundance over scarcity, and change over stagnation.

Positivity is the first building block.

Practicing positivity

 Positive Bias   Core Commitments

How can you encourage your team toward a positive mindset? Try this simple technique borrowed from the world of improvisational theater, where it's all about how you seize the material you are offered and run with it, build upon it, to make it greater.

Not every communication is perfect and complete on its own, but how you respond and expand on it can be either additive or contradictory. Feel the difference between the following responses:

"Yes, but…" versus "Yes, and…".

The first is an objection. It suggests the original speaker is incorrect, missing something fundamental, or needs to be contradicted. Whatever comes after the "but" will be perceived in that light, and as such is already colored by it.

An exactly identical response that instead follows a "Yes, and…" will feel completely different.

As a leader, you can model this in your team interactions and consciously practice it in an exercise. Try a simple starting-point statement and, working in pairs, your team can take turns responding to each other using either "Yes, and…" or "Yes, but…" — and they can then report back on where the conversation took them in each case, and how it makes them feel.

It can be challenging to step back and allow others the space to contribute, but if you don't, you'll never learn what they could add to a situation. When I was a young software developer, I rose to team leader and manager on the basis of competence — if something was right, it was usually my idea (or at least I thought so). As a result, if something was wrong, I was quick to point it out, and saw this as being decisive and effective. I didn't realize that every time I said no, I was teaching my team members to stop proposing ideas. By saying no, I was closing down my team's creative process.

It's all about shifting to an abundance mindset, where positivity feeds growth. When you replace negative words like "but" or "no" with "yes, and...", you open space for something new to take root. This leads to an abundance of ideas and possibilities.

Ask the inimitable Seth Godin:[1]

Yes, there's a free lunch

In a physical economy in which scarcity is the fundamental driver, eating lunch means someone else gets less.

But in a society where ideas lead to trust and connection and productivity, where working together is better than working apart, where exchange creates value for both sides...

Then the efficient sharing of ideas is its own free lunch. All of us are smarter than any of us, so the value to all goes up when you share.

---

1 http://sethgodin.typepad.com/seths_blog/2018/03/yes-theres-a-free-lunch.html

PART
THREE

The discipline
of freedom

When you are truly engaged in your work, in a state of flow, you don't have to think about your motivation. You don't think about what you could be doing instead, or how you feel about your choices — you're just immersed in the activity, and gaining great personal satisfaction from being optimally productive.

This is what every member of a high-performing team *should* be experiencing, but the reality is often a lot more messy and complex. When you have an expectation that everyone works fixed hours at a fixed location, for example, there can be huge variance in the extent to which each person is able to show up and perform, day after day, because of the complicated humans they are — never mind the complexities of the work itself. Just because a colleague is physically present, it doesn't mean they are emotionally in the same room or intellectually engaged with the work in hand. And that directly affects the work to be done.

So what does freedom mean in a high-performing team? In essence, it's the freedom to engage or disengage with the work, according to your inner state and effectiveness. Not to duck contractual obligations in terms of work responsibilities, but to have accepted that the way you best fulfill these is with an appropriate degree of autonomy and flexibility, to manage yourself and your level of contribution.

Team leaders need to exemplify this in their own behavior and can take a powerful role in modeling the acceptability of the protocols in this chapter. This is a direct antidote to the highly damaging possibility for martyred presenteeism, where team members feel they have to make a point of being at their desks when that's clearly the last place they ought to be.

Having the option to choose makes you take responsibility for your engagement and presence, and this is really powerful. If you find your mind wanders and you start checking or replying to email during a team meeting, would it be better to Check Out and concentrate on that email in

THE DISCIPLINE OF FREEDOM

another room? Or is this work meeting more important — in which case, how about closing the laptop and giving it your full attention for the duration? You explicitly choose whether to exit or to stay fully present, and this qualitatively enhances your presence and commitment. Try it and see.

Because you can't all be awesome all the time, there are tools to use to indicate this to your teammates whenever you need to:

Passing

The Pass protocol is a simple way to decline to participate in a conversation, activity, or decision.

It's a way of signaling your need to disengage clearly and unambiguously to your teammates, and you can use it at any time — even when an activity is underway. (The only exception to the "any time" rule, if you have adopted the Core Protocols in your team, is that you do need to participate in a Decider vote.) Simply saying "I pass" means you're out — by active choice. There's no need for drama or to physically exit the space; simply pass and your choice is made.

Once you're ready, unpass so that everyone knows you're back on it. Until then, while you remain physically present, keep quiet. You passed, so stay out of it.

Pass is a simple and powerful protocol you can easily experiment with in your teams by introducing the concept and then demonstrating its use in a couple of different situations. As a team leader, you can remind people they have this option in their toolkit if you spot any less-direct expressions of disengagement: "You look like you might want to pass on this…." Simple.

Of course, a team won't be effective if everyone passes on everything all the time, and this protocol should not be used as a way to avoid tough decisions or postpone difficult conversations. It's one of the simplest of the Core Protocols to get comfortable with as you work with your teams to make things better, but it's not a magic pill to avoid resolving conflict in a healthy way or to delay dealing with challenges — hence the Decider override indicated above. Some things you just have to show up for, whatever else is going on.

But at other times, you have choices and you can exercise them, thus allowing you to be fully present and engaged when ready to be so, and to be truly effective in your role of team member.

Checking out

The Check Out protocol can be seen as an extension of the Pass option we discussed above. Sometimes, opting out of a specific question or activity just isn't enough, and you need to signify withdrawal on a deeper level.

In high-performance teams, the physical presence (or virtual presence if distributed) of a colleague signifies that they're engaged and ready to contribute optimally. So the corollary expectation is that when this does not apply, you simply depart physically from the team space.

There's no need for explanation, drama, or disruption. Just state, "I'm checking out," and head for the door. Leave the room and everything going on in it until you're ready to return — then you check in, briefly and without fuss, to signify your readiness to be back on it.

Isn't that better than trying to work with people who are physically present yet everything about their body language, effort, or attention is signifying that their hearts and minds could not be further from the activity at hand? In a team of functioning and self-aware adults, this simply shouldn't be necessary, ever.

One of the hardest things for new adopters about using this protocol can be that it violates established behavioral norms around feelings that are commonplace in some teams or even communities. How often are we inclined to justify, apologize for, or try to explain our feelings, even if we feel okay to express them in the first place? If we don't feel psychologically safe in a workplace, sharing feelings creates vulnerability, and that creates fear.

As a leader, you can demonstrate the behaviors that the Check Out protocol involves, and also establish what it means in practice for your workplace. Do you need to actually leave the building, or does hitting a break room or separate space serve the purpose? Consider also how to manifest this protocol effectively on a distributed team — for example, logging out of the collaboration app or workspace, or simply turning off your video camera.

PART FOUR

Self-awareness: First, know what's going on for you

Of course, your team is not going to get a lot of work done unless people re-engage with it. That means taking ownership of your emotional state, and bringing it with you when you come to work.

Are you ready to be back in the room?

Unpass

The inverse of the Pass protocol is super simple. Once the conversation has moved on, or you have moved on internally, to the point where you're ready to be fully involved in it once more, just say, "I unpass."

There you are, back in the process — with no need to interrupt it, update people on your personal state, or explain your reasons for passing or unpassing. It's just like you've had your pause button pressed for a little while, and now you're disengaging the button.

That's got to be better than letting other people press your buttons, right?

But if you've been outside of the workspace or you're getting together at the start of a session, then you might need the stronger protocol of actually checking in — both with your colleagues and with yourself.

Checking in

When you're in a psychologically safe team environment, you bring your whole self into that space: your emotions, your thoughts, your distractions, and your physical state. We are complex chaotic humans, with all the baggage that entails.

You bring all that stuff to work with you, but on many teams, it isn't acknowledged. You may be expected to leave most of yourself at the door, only presenting the work-related thoughts and feelings. This ignores the impact that each person's contextual stuff has on the team's effectiveness and on the work itself — who can get their best work done when the room is full of everybody else's elephants?

The Check In protocol is a way to begin meetings or conversations by acknowledging your present state and sharing it with each other, in a simple declaration.

The team agreements that accompany Check In consist of:

- State your feelings without qualification — you don't need to justify or account for your state of mind. You can offer a brief explanation if you choose, in case it might be significant or there's important information the rest of the group is unaware of, but there's no requirement to do so. Nor should you diminish your emotions by using negative qualifiers, like saying you're "a little bit" sad.

- Talk only about your own feelings — it's not a moment to reflect or interpret or relate to anyone else present, or how anyone has "made" you feel. A little bit of context is fine, but keep it about you and how you feel.

- Listen respectfully while others are checking in.

- Do not discuss or refer to another person's check-in unless invited to do so or given explicit permission.

Under the Core Protocols, a check-in is short and sweet, because you express all emotions in terms using the four primary emotions: glad, sad, mad, and afraid. (It's fine to substitute "happy" for "glad" or "scared" for "afraid" if that language seems more comfortable.)

By combining these primary emotions, you can express more complex states. For example, excitement may be a combination of glad and afraid while feelings of loss may be a mix of mad and sad. Using these four primary emotions really helps you check in with yourself first to accurately know and define your personal state. With a little forethought, you can check in profoundly with just these four words, and the process provides an instant update for your colleagues that isn't dependent on vocabulary or nuance. When you do a check-in by the book, you conclude with the phrase "I'm in."

In many teams familiar with and using the Core Protocols, it's habitual for everyone to check in if one person does so. This is how high-performing teams stay up to date with everyone's present state: they frequently and immediately perform a temperature check of the team. With some practice, it can be done quickly, even in a large group. So it means creating a habit of awareness of your own emotional state (which I will explore in more depth below) and being able to rapidly categorize this, as a quick signifier for colleagues. Being in touch with your own feelings is an asset in any situation.

A high-performing team leader will rapidly identify the impact of the team's check-ins on their effectiveness and productivity, and how the depth of disclosure that occurs at the outset breaks down the barriers between individuals and facilitates a level of emotional intimacy that is appropriate for a high-performing team. Conversely, you will also quickly identify the negative outcomes when someone has not checked in fully or effectively, and thus is out of sync with the rest of the team.

Personal Alignment

As a leader, you will only get the best from others if you are your own best self. And performing at your best is greatly assisted by knowing yourself well.

The Personal Alignment protocol can help you dig deeply into your own desires and unlock the underlying motivations. But just knowing this is only the first step. You then need to remove the barriers by invoking the personal qualities that will clear them from your path.

It's an introspective process, but you can involve others when you need to. Leaders who show vulnerabilities in this way also build trust.

But it starts with you, and asking yourself three simple questions:

1. What do I want? Be very specific.
2. What is blocking me from having what I want?
3. What virtue, if I had it, would help me shatter this block?

Then think about that virtue, that personal quality. You need to have it, to master it, in order to move on. Ergo, that quality is the thing you *really* want! Repeat the questions, this time using the identified virtue as the answer to question one. You might have to run through the cycle of "what virtue would get me to what I truly want and need right now?" several times. You'll know once you get there.

This process will help you arrive at a unique, specific personal virtue that is going to unlock your potential. This is your personal alignment statement, which you can write down in the format, "I want [self-awareness/passion/integrity/courage/etc.]."

You can then share this with your colleagues, and ask them to help you practice specific behaviors or responses that will help you work toward your personal alignment. You can decide on a specific signal that indicates your goal to others on your team: "Right now I am working on my courage. Will you help me to extend myself, and work towards this goal? If you sense a cop-out or notice that I am taking a less courageous path to a decision or action, will you call me on it?" (Of course, they may not always be ready to help in the way requested, but that's fine too — see "Asking for help," below.)

What gets measured gets managed, so set yourself specific activity assignments and targets. To get your unconscious behaviors congruent with your desired alignment, you will have to deliberately modify what you do at first, perhaps for a while. Celebrate your accomplishments by reflecting on your successful changes.

Best results will always come to you when you identify the big wins, so don't be afraid to tackle the blocks that, if solved, would make the biggest difference to your effectiveness and happiness in aspects of your life. This might be pretty deep-rooted and it could take several iterations of the self-reflection process above but it's well worth the outcome. And don't be afraid to share that outcome with the team that helped you get there.

Maybe it's difficult to identify that block and put a label on it. In that case, you can ask for help from others. Bear in mind that a personal block is something internal; it's not about circumstances or events or other people. So it means owning your own response to external factors and working out what that is triggering within you. That's the only thing you can work on and change.

If you are the team leader, modeling this process will not only help your colleagues understand you better, it will deepen the connection between you all. And you will demonstrate clearly to them that change, if they want it for themselves, is within their own grasp. Being open about your intentions, signposting what you are doing to achieve the shift, and then sharing your success and what it means to you will encourage everyone to examine and pursue their own most fundamental personal alignments — and this will have a direct impact on the quality of your results as a team.

You can even share the results as a ceremony or celebration. And never forget, when you're part of a team, you're not on your own — your colleagues are there for the highs and the lows.

One of the remarkable things about focusing some thinking time on your personal alignment is that you will come across more opportunities to practice and perfect it, just because of this reflection. The abundance of the universe will deliver the goods, via the cognitive bias known as the Baader-Meinhof phenomenon, or recency illusion — you'll suddenly start to notice everywhere unexpected incidences of the thing you have been focusing on! Just as when you're thinking about a possible new travel destination, for example, or a new car to buy, you start to find it coming up in conversations or reading apparently all over the place. Of course, those references were there all along, in your crowded life. But where your mind has been (consciously or otherwise) is where your attention goes.

Asking for help

When people come together to collaborate, you end up with something greater than the sum of its parts. Synergy happens, ideas procreate, and abundant new things develop. Different people bring different strengths, virtues, and experiences to the table. Teammates can help you practice your personal alignment, and they can help you solve problems and progress toward your goals in a multitude of ways.

You just have to ask. And sometimes we're not good at that, which is why the Core Protocols make it explicitly okay and indeed actively encourage asking for help. You can do this before, during, and after the pursuit of any result; there's no fixed window of intervention. The Ask for Help protocol helps you leverage the shared resources of the team by making it safe to ask, to define the kind of help you need, and for the helper to respond with yes or no as they see fit.

To use the protocol well, it's essential that you understand exactly what help you want. Of course, it's okay to ask for help in clarifying your needs and ideas first if that's where you're stuck, but it's most respectful to your proposed helper if you do your own thinking first and get your query into as tight a shape as possible.

For this protocol to work, there has to be an absolute understanding that your potential helper can agree to help or not with complete freedom. In fact, they have a total responsibility to say no if they're not able to fully engage with the request for any reason. They should no more apologize for declining to assist than the asker should apologize for requesting help — neither party needs justification, reward, or emotional drama. There's no quid pro quo; you are a team working on common goals. This is a peer-to-peer engagement that may be different from an assignment or instruction given to you by a manager.

It shouldn't be a big deal to ask for help, and then either receive it or not. You should do it early enough in a process, before a challenge becomes a crisis, and you should be open to clarifying questions and exploration. Whatever the outcome of the request and response, it's a team interaction that is positive and communicates something about what you're working on and thinking about. It might even help you think it through for yourself after all, meaning no help is needed.

PART FIVE

Teamwork depends on connection

All of the activities outlined so far are demonstrations of how to connect with others, in the context of managing our own internal state. When you work in a team, you are in two states simultaneously: a self-contained individual with your own emotions and motivations and a part of a greater whole. Managing that boundary between self and team requires consciously reaching across it in a variety of ways.

Intention Check

It's important to remain aware that however close you feel to your team members, however well aligned and checked in with them you have become, you are still an individual with your own internal world. Everyone is. As such, your understanding of why others behave in the way that they do is informed by a combination of signals, such as:

- your expectations and attribution errors;
- their past behavior;
- their work-related objectives and goals, including shared objectives;
- their present emotional state (which they might have recently shared with you via a check-in); and
- external factors such as project constraints, deadlines and the presence of others.

So you can see that however close you are as a team, however well you know that person as an individual, you're outside their head and basically guessing, trying to triangulate a motivation for them from a variety of factors, which are bound to be incomplete on some level.

Consequently, you sometimes need to clarify your understanding of someone else's intent, particularly if you observe that the way they are behaving might violate a Core Protocol or some other team norm or if you can't foresee their course of action having a positive outcome. You might have fundamental concerns about their integrity or be confused about what they're doing or the way they're going about it — use the Intention Check protocol to get the clarity you need.

Equally, regardless of formal leadership roles within the team, it's perfectly okay for someone to check on your intentions, whenever they feel the need — for them to ask you, "What is your intention with X?" where X is some kind of actual or pending behavior or action.

If it's relevant and helpful, you can intention-check a previous event as well, by asking, "What response or behavior did you want [from whom] as a result of X?" If you have a problem with the consequences of somebody's action, you first inquire whether that was the outcome they expected so that you can learn from their intent, actions, and actual results.

It's not surprising that the Intention Check protocol might spring to mind at points of high tension or conflict within the team. So make no mistake: this is *not* designed to be used to call people out, shame them, or draw attention to their mistakes to make yourself or others look good. It stands to reason therefore that you need to be completely clear about your own intentions before invoking the protocol. Will this enhance connectedness and understanding within the team? Will it help us do things differently another time if something has spectacularly screwed up? Or am I just badly in need of a vent for my own emotions?

You *cannot* conduct an intention check if you are angry, defensive, or frustrated, so you'll have to defer it if your own feelings are triggered. Calmly and constructively inquiring what intention was behind a specific action is a world away from "What the XXXX did you think would happen if you did that!?" If you have to resolve your own emotions first, it's better to check out and do so.

If you have a fundamental problem with a team member's actions, and that cannot be defused by the simple time-out buffer that checking out provides for, remember that it's always a good practice to ask for help. Perhaps it's a pattern of behavior, of cause and effect, that you're observing between you and another person. Someone else on the team might be aware of it before you are and well placed to help you reflect upon it and resolve it, or you might need to involve someone completely external to the whole situation. Either way, you need to sort it out.

A good leader recognizes that on a team of individuals who bring their whole unique selves to the workplace, some degree of disagreement, of creative tension, is not only inevitable, it is in fact a good thing. When ideas and suggestions are open to challenge and investigation, it's a way to make them stronger, as well as to increase our resilience. Ideas become products that go out and get tested in the real world, so it stands to reason that testing is a vital part of this process. In the end, the measure of a team's performance is its results.

Investigate

Potential misunderstandings often can be preempted well before any need to call someone's intentions into question by merely showing curiosity and interest in what they're doing and by understanding what drives them in the first place. It's sometimes too easy to work alongside someone day after day, each doing your own thing in your own way, and observing and understanding relatively little of what they're doing, simply because you're working on different things.

The Investigate protocol lets you clarify an idea or behavior you might find confusing, inappropriate, or even fascinating. All you do is ask questions as a detached but fascinated inquirer, probing and clarifying until you resolve your curiosity.

You should only use this protocol when your own motives are authentic and transparent. "Seek first to understand."[1] If you go in with your own agenda, and you're not investigating but looking for justification, evidence, or ammunition... — stop! Avoid confirmation bias and leading questions.

Simple, direct questions are best. As with asking for help, respect your colleague's time by thinking first and then asking questions that are well thought out and take account of what has already been shared and discussed. The point of the dialogue — which is what it should be, rather than any kind of interrogation — is to increase your understanding.

Assuming their time is not under pressure and they have no reason to mistrust your intent, people frequently enjoy talking about themselves and their work. Simple, direct questions tend to form the most effective investigations, so use those rather than encouraging them to tell stories. Probe for depth, and explore specifics: what about the situation makes

---

1   https://www.stephencovey.com/7habits/7habits-habit5.php

that happen, what outcome do you want, what's the biggest obstacle, what do you need? Can you give me a specific example?

The one thing you must do is maintain your detached position, and do *not* offer your own opinions. Keep your questions and follow-up probing to neutral, unloaded language — it's actually a great exercise in asking clean questions well and exploring the power of fascination and curiosity.

If you're desperate to respond to the person you're investigating and to interject with your own opinions, then it might not be the best time to investigate that person. Intention-check yourself first and check out for a bit if that's what is needed.

If you feel that you're being misunderstood or perhaps that a contribution or activity is undervalued or the relevance to broader goals is unclear, then invite team members to investigate you. This is an example of the Ask for Help protocol in action: "Will you investigate me about X?" This not only helps the team get clarity about what you're doing, but it might also resolve some unexpressed thoughts in your own mind.

And should a colleague initiate this activity spontaneously, it's an excellent opportunity for you as a leader to demonstrate how to respond: with gratitude for their curiosity, enthusiasm for your work, and thoughtful responsiveness to their inquiry. You can be a role model for how to be investigated constructively and efficiently, without defensiveness or negativity, and instead confirm this as an opportunity for both parties to grow and learn from one another.

PART SIX

Productivity and high performance

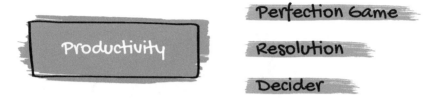

High-performing teams get stuff done. They don't get hung up in indecision or fail to move things forward. The Core Protocols provide specific tools to make decisions, unstick difficulties, and drive unanimity and consensus.

Calling a Decider

Many minds are better than one when it comes to finding solutions and making progress, and the goal of the team is to work with the best ideas at all times.

As Jim McCarthy said, "The goal in any product design is to have the best ideas become the basis of the product. Everybody on the team should be working to accomplish that goal."[1]

New ideas might require changes, but one thing that can potentially hinder groups is the need to make decisions and changes. Differences of opinion can delay action, and the Decider protocol exists to simplify and speed up this process.

It should be used for simple, concrete, single-item actions. The more complex you make your proposal, the more difficult it is to get unanimous support for it. Instead of gargantuan complex proposals, try making simple proposals and decisions, and adding on to them with a sequence of additional simple proposals and decisions.

It goes like this:

---

1 Jim McCarthy, *Dynamics of Software Development* by Jim McCarthy, Denis Gilbert, ISBN: 1556158238

- A proposer says, "I propose [the action/change]," and counts down "1, 2, 3."

- Voters respond by raising their hand, either yes (thumb up), no (thumb down), or "support it" (flat hand).

- If a voter absolutely cannot agree with the proposal, they should immediately declare this by stating they are an "absolute no" and that they won't get in. The Decider is about moving forward with consensus, so this stops the flow, and the proposer withdraws the proposal.

- Assuming no "absolute no" deal-breakers, the proposer counts the votes. The proposer is looking for all yes and "support it" votes, with a majority of yes votes.

- If required, the Resolution protocol is invoked to engage dissenters.

- The proposer declares the proposal carried if the dissenters get behind it.

- The *whole* team is now committed to the proposed change.

This is an incredibly rapid activity that can save an incredible amount of otherwise wasted time that frequently derails group activities. "It's getting late. I propose we push on until 12:30, and if we're not done, we take a 10-minute breather then order pizza. One, two, three…. Decided." And it works because you only move forward on decisions for which you have unanimous consensus: everyone explicitly supports the proposal or supports the team's decision on the proposal.

When to use Resolution

Of course, not all proposals pass unanimously. In a team of high emotional intelligence, people feel comfortable expressing dissenting views via the "no" vote. While the team unit needs to have a bias to action as part of the positivity that underpins the base of the high-performance building blocks, consensus about any particular proposal isn't a given. It is the ability to synthesize the diverse presented viewpoints that makes the team great.

Resolution is needed when anyone on the team votes no during a Decider. The Resolution protocol is a drive toward consensus, simply asking each dissenting voter to clarify what it would it take to get them in. This gives them the opportunity to contribute to the idea, to grow it: "Yes, and…!" Sometimes, a proposal is needed in principle but can be refined and polished by team input. Exploring and investigating it as a team can make it even greater without diluting the original need.

Of course, the time and effort of the resolution process depend on the significance of the proposal overall, and choice of pizza versus sushi is probably not worth an epic debate. But as a team leader, you could use a low-stakes decision like this to walk through the process and explore how your team investigates and resolves each other's choices in a consensual way.

For effective resolution, a dissenting teammate should be able to respond in a single, declarative statement with the exact modification to the proposal it would take to get them on board. They don't need to explain or justify why they voted no. The purpose is to add to the proposal and make it better — to state precisely what it will take to get them to back it, to be wholeheartedly "in".

The modification to the proposal will usually enhance and strengthen it under the "many minds" principle; as such, it is unlikely to impact the resolve of other team members, and the proposer can make a simple eye check to ensure continued consensus. However, it's possible, given the diversity and synergy of the group, that a modification might significantly alter or amend the proposal to the extent that it needs to be reworked because people's responses to it may have changed or developed. In this case, the proposer should withdraw the original proposal and then submit a new one taking the modifications into account with a second Decider.

Good Deciders lead to good decisions

Because Decider is a fast, positive, and immediate protocol, there are a number of factors required to make it happen well.

The first is a well-formed proposal. If you want to put something to the team, think it through first and make sure it truly is a single decision that people can respond to with a yes or a no. If a proposal is too weak to be expressed clearly, it should be withdrawn and worked on until it's better.

Deciders are essential, and the team needs to be ready for a Decider at any time. You do not get to pass during a Decider; this is the only protocol in which a pass is disallowed. Your vote counts; even if your vote is "support the team's decision", you are part of the decision and you are responsible for carrying it out. You owe it to your teammates to give a Decider your full attention, to pause in whatever else you are doing until the decision is made — it generally won't take long. (The corollary to this is that the proposer is aware they are interrupting the work, breaking everybody's flow, and won't do so unless they genuinely feel that the potential gains from the outcome make this a price worth paying.)

The proposer is the only one who speaks, unless they invite someone else to do so by way of resolution or informal clarification or a voter needs to declare an absolute no. If you are not in the "absolute no" category, you respond with your hands, not your mouth, and the protocol is to do so immediately on the count of three. Never mind what other people are doing; it's only your response you are responsible for. Keep your reasons to yourself — there is something quite powerful about responding with a hand signal instead of words, which might help inhibit that urge to explain, justify, apologize, or undermine your immediate and instinctive response.

Interrupting with an absolute no doesn't require apology either, but it does mean you need to share your thoughts and ideas with the group. The Core Commitments contain an explicit bias to action, and you are halting that action — which is fine, provided there's a reason, and ideally a better idea. For whatever reason, you did not get around to proposing your idea first, so now you need to crystalize it fast and get it out there so the team can examine it and understand exactly why you couldn't get behind the original proposal no matter what.

It's those last three words — "no matter what" — that put the absolute no beyond the possibility of resolution, and as such this response should be used as rarely as possible, and with sensitivity and discretion.

Think of your absolute no as a direct cost to the team in terms of its forward momentum and productivity. Is your objection worth this cost? If it is, articulate it clearly. It's the responsibility of every member of a high-performing team to follow their instinct, conscience, or whatever drives this response through to its fully examined conclusion.

It follows, though, that you shouldn't exercise this procedure lightly, and definitely not in the following circumstances:

- Do not "absolute no" when you are unclear about precisely what is being proposed. Remember that after this Decider, you can always propose a modification or add-on, and if you are simply in a position of misunderstanding, you can later seek clarification from the proposer. Perhaps you are missing some background information, but something happening while you were checked out or not paying attention is not a reason to break the team's forward momentum. Remember, you can always make an additional or alternative proposal later on after you have gotten clarity. In a high-performing team, you can be confident that they will *always* support the strongest and best idea, whenever it emerges.

- Do not "absolute no" when you have ideas that only marginally improve the proposal. Don't break the team's bias toward positive action with an objection just because you can see a way to make it even better! You can make an additional proposal after the current one or you can make sure you're involved in implementing the new idea and contribute your ideas at the appropriate time. Remember, "Yes, AND..." — keep the synergistic improvements coming at all times.

Once the decision has passed, it becomes part of your team agreements, and therefore your own responsibility to the team. That's why you cannot pass on being involved, and your objection may need to be resolved — because once it's done, it's done. The time to debate and express reservations has passed; you are now committed to the outcome. In the absence of any new information or changed circumstances, the same proposal should not come up for a Decider again once the team has made up its collective mind.

As such, you also have a responsibility to update yourself about any Decider commitments made when you are absent or checked out. You are part of a team that has made a decision, and you're committed to working unceasingly towards that deliverable.

This protocol is one where it might be necessary to focus attention on the detail of the process, and insist on adherence to it. We all have a natural tendency to campaign, to persuade, to canvas support, and try to influence others — but this is not the time or place for that. The Core Protocols are written in simple language to make them easy to follow and fall back on, and if you need to be the one who reminds others about this or even insists upon it, then so be it.

And as the proposer, remember that you are breaking the team's flow and altering the direction of the work, so make sure you're doing it for a good reason, with a strong and clear proposition that will move things forward and make them better. If you misjudge the moment — for example, if a proposal receives less than two-thirds support — then it's better to promptly withdraw it and rethink it. Perhaps it needs a bit more work, it's too radical a change, or you simply need to investigate where others are at to understand their perspective. Either way, the best way to support the team is probably not to try to resolve it at that point, with so little consensus.

Finally, this protocol's speed and effectiveness rely on being able to view and count the response in the group rapidly and accurately. As such, it's best with smaller numbers. If there are a number of decisions to be made, perhaps they could be delegated to smaller break-out teams, who report back to the full team. This might be the best way to move the team through a number of complex sticking points. Everyone who is checked in and available collaborates to decide on the proposals that affect them. If the team members were unavailable and checked out, they explicitly support their teammates' decisions and abide by them.

Perfection Game

Being awesome is a journey, not a destination. Perfection is what we continually move toward, in ourselves and within our teams. We are not machines on a production line; we are human beings, always growing and learning, and always with the potential to improve. As such, we can always welcome input to help us optimize, expand, and better ourselves.

The Perfection Game protocol exists to help you surface the best ideas within your teams. It's a choice to engage with teammates; sometimes, you know exactly what we need to do to make things better but other times it helps to actively solicit input from those with an external perspective and new ideas to offer. You should use this protocol to focus on something you have created and that you want to make even better.

To use the protocol, ask someone to be your perfector. The perfector's role is to gauge how much value they personally can add to a product/ creation. They then rate the value of the object or performance on a scale of 1 to 10 based *on how much value they can add,* not on their perceived absolute value of the object itself.

If the perfector perceives significant flaws with an output but honestly cannot see how to put it right in any way, then they must rate it a 10. They are not invited to critique, judge, or say what they don't like, only to add to the product/creation and make it better. This is important, because it allows the Perfection Game to be subjective yet free from judgment.

Perfectors should frame their review positively, starting with what they liked or valued about the creation. They can then follow by saying, "To make it a 10 for me, you'd have to do X."

The flow of the protocol is important here. We don't jump in by insulting our teammate or stating what we hate about their creation; that will teach them not to ask for help. Instead, you emphasize what is good within the work and propose an improvement and a clear path to the better outcome you are suggesting.

Putting numbers on it helps you clarify the strength of the recommendation you are making. If you believe your suggestions will make one aspect of the object twice as good, then it's okay to rate the object as a 5/10. This will encourage you as the perfector to be detailed and explicit about exactly what needs to be done to perfect and improve, avoiding woolly, subjective, or vague feedback in favor of specific ideas and suggestions.

As the perfectee, remember that you solicited this feedback out of a genuine desire to improve what you're doing. You don't need to defend your decisions or respond to the feedback; it is, after all, up to you whether or not act on the improvement ideas. When you ask more than one person to perfect your work, you might receive advice that appears to be contradictory. In an abundant creative environment, though, there is no such thing as contradiction — there are only ideas which combine and grow and may spark something entirely new instead.

So whatever they contribute, your perfectors deserve your thanks for playing the game with you, and for helping you be incrementally more awesome.

PART
SEVEN

Staying aligned through effective error handling

The Core Protocols were originally derived from observing software development teams, and one thing that every developer learns early in their career is the critical importance of debugging. Checking, testing, and correcting course as needed is a vital part of the workflow. It is anticipated, budgeted for, and performed without judgment. The 11th of the Core Commitments requires team members not to do dumb things on purpose, but in a complex, fast-moving creative process, mistakes inevitably happen.

The good thing about being part of a team that has adopted the Core Protocols, however, is that mistakes can be corrected at any stage, before they become significant problems which could take the project off course in a big way. It reflects the agile fail-fast, learn-fast, improve-fast idea, in which you can be pick up and deal with any errors early instead of waiting to measure outcomes at some distant endpoint.

Protocol Check

All Protocol Check means in practice is that any member of the team can call for one at any point in any activity if they believe that a Core Commitment is not being kept or that a protocol is being misused in some way.

Just say "protocol check" and share the correct use of the protocol if known, or simply voice your uncertainty and ask others for help to clarify what's going on.

Don't hesitate, regardless of what you are in the middle of. Mistakes in direction always get magnified as time passes, so a misalignment takes you further and further from the right course.

Ask for help as soon as you realize you're unsure of the correct protocol use but don't hide behind lack of clarity if you know perfectly well which protocol is being broken. Don't be passive-aggressive. State clearly what is going on, without fear of punishment or shame. Know that your colleagues will support you, as you would do the same for them. You all share the objective of great work output, and this is best served by keeping your Core Commitments and observing the protocols to which you have committed.

Anyone on the team can perform a protocol check at any point, regardless of institutional role or hierarchy — in fact, on a high-performing team, every person has a direct responsibility to do so and to call out any behavior they observe that damages the team and the work you are doing together.

On high-performing teams, leaders acknowledge and support protocol checks at any point, and use them as learning and improvement opportunities for the whole team.

It's all part of continually getting better and better.

PART EIGHT

Conclusions and next steps

Diagnostics

Measure your teams' effectiveness across many dimensions:

- Performance
- High-performance Behaviors
- Team Emotional Itelligence
- Agility

Understand the current state of your organization

Create your path to high performance

Training & Coaching

1-2 day courses:

- High-Performance Teams:

  Core Protocols for Psychological Safety and El

- Agile & Scrum Foundations
- Agile Product Owner Skills
- Agile Technical Skills

5-day course:

- Core Protocols Boot Camp

Coaching on high-performance team behaviors

Repeat

- Re-measure your teams every 3-4 months
- Tune subsequent trainig, coaching, and practice as you continue on your path to a high-performance organization

Your Path to a High-performance Organization

Practice Groups

Weekly group sessions to grow your new skills

Trainer Certification

Master the skills by becoming a certified trainer

Scale the program by training your own trainers

41

If you have found this introduction to the Core Protocols valuable in your work and you want to deepen your practice and skill set for leading your own team, then I invite you to learn more.

Visit kasperowski.com to:

- Read our blog.

- Listen to the With Great People podcast.

- Use one of our diagnostics to gauge your team's performance and understand where to improve.

- Find out about live events and workshops. By far the best way to extend your learning and improve your personal practice as both a team leader and team member is to attend a live event, either in person or online. These events will also equip you with activities, games, and processes you can take straight back to your team and put into action.

- Participate in our weekly online practice group. Become a certified trainer.

For now, thank you for reading *High-Performance Teams: The Foundations*. We wish you greatness in everything you do.

APPENDIX

The Core Protocols[1]

The following Core Protocols are made up of both commitments and protocols.

The Core Commitments

1. I commit to engage when present.
    a. To know and disclose
        i. what I want,
        ii. what I think, and
        iii. what I feel.

    b. To always seek effective help.

    c. To decline to offer and refuse to accept incoherent emotional transmissions.

    d. When I have or hear a better idea than the currently prevailing idea, I will immediately
        i. propose it for decisive acceptance or rejection and/or
        ii. explicitly seek its improvement.

    e. I will personally support the best idea
        i. regardless of its source,
        ii. however much I hope an even better idea may later arise, and
        iii. when I have no superior alternative idea.

2. I will seek to perceive more than I seek to be perceived.

3. I will use teams, especially when undertaking difficult tasks.

---

1 The Core Protocols version 3.1 is copyright © 2018 Richard Kasperowski

Version 3.1 of the Core Protocols is derived from the Core Protocols version 3.03 by Jim and Michele McCarthy. This derivation improves the readability of version 3.03.

The Core Protocols version 3.03 is copyright © 2010 Jim and Michele McCarthy

(The Core is distributed under the terms of the GNU General Public License as published by the Free Software Foundation, either version 3 of the License, or (at your option) any later version. For exact terms see http://www.gnu.org/licenses/. The Core is considered as source code under that agreement. You are free to use and distribute this work or any derivations you care to make, provided you also distribute this source document in its entirety, including this paragraph.)

4. I will speak always and only when I believe it will improve the general results/effort ratio.

5. I will offer and accept only rational, results-oriented behavior and communication.

6. I will disengage from less productive situations
    a. when I cannot keep these commitments and
    b. when it is more important that I engage elsewhere.

7. I will do now what must be done eventually and can effectively be done now.

8. I will seek to move forward toward a particular goal by biasing my behavior toward action.

9. I will use the Core Protocols (or better) when applicable.
    a. I will offer and accept timely and proper use of the Protocol Check protocol without prejudice.

10. I will neither harm — nor tolerate the harming of — anyone for his or her fidelity to these commitments.

11. I will never do anything dumb on purpose.

The Core Protocols

Pass (Unpass)

The Pass protocol is how you decline to participate in something. Use it anytime you don't want to participate in an activity.

Steps

1. When you've decided not to participate, say "I pass."

2. Unpass any time you desire. Unpass as soon as you know you want to participate again by saying "I unpass."

Commitments

- Hold reasons for passing private.

- Pass on something as soon as you are aware you are going to pass.

- Respect the right of others to pass without explanation.

- Support those who pass by not discussing them or their pass.

- Do not judge, shame, hassle, interrogate, or punish anyone who passes.

Notes

- In general, you will not be in good standing with your Core Commitments if you pass most of the time.

- You can pass on any activity; however, if you have adopted the Core Commitments, you cannot pass on a Decider vote and you must say "I'm in" when checking in.

- You can pass even though you have already started something.

Check In

Use the Check In protocol to begin meetings or anytime an individual or group check-in would add more value to the current team interactions.

Steps

1. Speaker says "I feel [one or more of mad, sad, glad, afraid]." Speaker may provide a brief explanation. If others have already checked in, the speaker may say "I pass." (See the Pass protocol.)

2. Speaker says "I'm in." This signifies that the speaker intends to behave according to the Core Commitments.

3. Listeners respond "Welcome."

Commitments

•   State feelings without qualification.

•   State feelings only as they pertain to yourself.

•   Be silent during another's check-in.

•   Do not refer to another's check-in disclosures without explicitly granted permission from him or her.

Notes

•   In the context of the Core Protocols, all emotions are expressed through combinations of mad, sad, glad, or afraid. For example, "excited" may be a combination of glad and afraid.

•   Check in as deeply as possible. Checking in with two or more emotions is the norm. The depth of a group's check-in translates directly to the quality of the group's results.

•   Do not do anything to diminish your emotional state. Do not describe yourself as a "little" mad, sad, glad, or afraid, or say "I'm mad, but I'm still glad."

•   Except in large groups, if more than one person checks in, it is recommended that all do so.

•   "Happy" may be substituted for "glad" and "scared" may be substituted for "afraid".

Check Out

The Check Out protocol requires that your physical presence always signifies your engagement. You must check out when you are aware that you cannot maintain the Core Commitments or whenever it would be better for you to be elsewhere.

Steps

1. Say "I'm checking out."

2. Physically leave the group until you're ready to check in once again.

3. Optionally, if it is known and relevant, you can say when you believe you'll return.

4. Those who are present for the check-out may not follow the person, talk to or talk about the person checking out, or otherwise chase him or her.

Commitments

- Return as soon as you can and are able to keep the Core Commitments.

- Return and check in without unduly calling attention to your return.

- Do not judge, shame, hassle, interrogate, or punish anyone who checks out.

Notes

- When you check out, do it as calmly and gracefully as possible so as to cause minimal disruption to others.

- Check out if your emotional state is hindering your success, if your receptivity to new information is too low, or if you do not know what you want.

- Checking out is an admission that you are unable to contribute at the present time.

Ask for Help

The Ask for Help protocol allows you to efficiently make use of the skills and knowledge of others. Ask for Help is the act that catalyzes connection and shared vision. Use it continually, before and during the pursuit of any result.

Steps

1. Asker inquires of another, "[Helper's name], will you X?"

2. Asker expresses any specifics or restrictions of the request.

3. Helper responds by saying yes or no, or by offering an alternative form of help.

Commitments

*   Always invoke the Ask for Help Protocol with the phrase "Will you ... ?"

*   Have a clear understanding of what you want from the helper, or if you do not have a clear understanding of what help you want, signal this by saying, "I'm not sure what I need help with, but will you help me?"

*   Assume that all helpers are always available and trust that any helper accepts the responsibility to say no.

*   Say no any time you do not want to help.

*   Accept the answer "no" without any inquiry or emotional drama.

*   Be receptive of the help offered.

*   Offer your best help even if it is not what the asker is expecting.

*   Postpone the help request if you are unable to fully engage.

*   Request more information if you are unclear about the specifics of the help request.

*   Do not apologize for asking for help.

Notes

- Asking for help is a low-cost undertaking. The worst possible outcome is a "no," which leaves you no further ahead or behind than when you asked. In the best possible outcome, you reduce the amount of time required to achieve a task and/or learn.

- Helpers should say no if they are not sure if they want to help. They should say nothing else after turning down a request for help.

- You cannot "over-ask" a given person for help unless he or she has asked you to respect a particular limit.

- If you don't understand the value of what is offered, feel that it wouldn't be useful, or believe that you already have considered and rejected the idea offered previously, assume a curious stance instead of executing a knee-jerk "But..." rejection. (See the Investigate protocol.)

- Asking in times of trouble means you waited too long to ask for help. Ask for help when you are doing well.

- Simply connecting with someone, even if he or she knows nothing of the subject you need help on, can help you find answers within yourself, especially if you ask that person to investigate you.

Protocol Check

Use a protocol check when you believe a protocol is being used incorrectly in any way, or when a Core Commitment is being broken.

Steps

1. Say "Protocol check."

2. If you know the correct use of the protocol, state it. If you don't, ask for help.

Commitments

• Say "protocol check" as soon as you become aware of the incorrect use of a protocol, or of a broken Core Commitment. Do this regardless of the current activity.

• Be supportive of anyone using protocol check.

• Do not shame or punish anyone using protocol check.

• Ask for help as soon as you realize you are unsure of the correct protocol use.

Intention Check

Use an Intention Check to clarify the purpose of your own or another's behavior. Use it when you expect current behavior to result in other than a positive outcome. Intention Check assesses the integrity of your own or another's intention in a given case.

Steps

1. Ask the person whose intention you want to know "What is your/my intention with X?", where X equals some type of actual or pending behavior.

2. If it would be helpful, ask "What response or behavior did you want from whom as a result of X?"

Commitments

• Be aware of your own intention before checking the intention of another.

• Investigate sufficiently to uncover the intention of the person or his actions.

• Make sure you have the intention to resolve any possible conflict peacefully before intention-checking someone else. If you do not have a peaceful intention, check out.

• Do not be defensive when someone asks you what your intention is. If you can't do this, check out.

Notes

• If conflict arises that seems irresolvable, check out and ask for help.

Decider

Use the Decider protocol anytime you want to move a group immediately and unanimously towards results.

Steps

1.   Proposer says "I propose [concise, actionable behavior]."

2.   Proposer counts "1, 2, 3."

3.   Voters, using either yes (thumbs up), no (thumbs down), or "support it" (flat hand), and vote simultaneously with other voters.

4.   Voters who absolutely cannot get in on the proposal declare themselves by saying "I am an absolute no. I won't get in." If this occurs, the proposal is withdrawn.

5.   Proposer counts the votes.

6.   Proposer withdraws the proposal if the total of dissenters (no votes) and "support it" votes is too great or if the proposer expects not to successfully conclude resolution (below). You can approximate "too great" by using the following heuristics:

   a. approximately 50 percent (or more) of votes are "support it" or

   b. the anticipated gain if the proposal passes is less than the likely cost of resolution effort.

7.   Proposer uses the Resolution protocol with each dissenter to bring him or her in by asking "What will it take to get you in?"

8.   Proposer declares the proposal carried if all dissenters change their votes to yes or "support it".

9.   The team is now committed to the proposed result.

Commitments

•   Propose no more than one item per proposal.

•   Remain present until the Decider protocol is complete; always remain aware of how your behavior either moves the group forward or slows it down.

- Give your full attention to a proposal over and above all other activity.

- Speak only when you are the proposer or are directed to speak by the proposer.

- Keep the reasons you voted as you did to yourself during the protocol.

- Reveal immediately when you are an absolute-no voter and be ready to propose a better idea.

- Be personally accountable for achieving the results of a Decider commitment even if it was made in your absence.

- Keep informed about Decider commitments made in your absence.

- Do not argue with an absolute-no voter. Always ask him or her for a better idea.

- Actively support the decisions reached.

- Use your capacity to "stop the show" by declaring you "won't get in no matter what" with great discretion and as infrequently as possible.

- Insist at all times that the Decider and Resolution protocols be followed exactly as per specification, regardless of how many times you find yourself doing the insisting.

- Do not pass during a decider.

- Unceasingly work toward forward momentum; have a bias toward action.

- Do not look at how others are voting to choose your own vote.

- Avoid using decider in large groups. Break up into small subgroups to make decisions, and use the large group to report status.

Notes

- Vote no only when you really believe the contribution to forward momentum you will make to the group after slowing or stopping it in the current vote will greatly outweigh the (usually considerable) costs you are adding by voting no.

- If you are unsure or confused by a proposal, support it and seek clarification offline after the proposal is resolved. If you have an alternate proposal after receiving more information, you can have faith that your team will support the best idea. (See "The Core Commitments.")

- Voting no to make minor improvements to an otherwise acceptable proposal slows momentum and should be avoided. Instead, offer an additional proposal after the current one passes or, better yet, involve yourself in the implementation to make sure your idea gets in.

- Withdraw weak proposals. If a proposal receives less than 70 percent (approximately) yes votes, it is a weak proposal and should be withdrawn by the proposer. This decision is, however, at the discretion of the proposer.

- Think of yourself as a potential solo outlier every time you vote no.

- Vote absolute no only when you are convinced you have a significant contribution to make to the direction or leadership of the group, or when integrity absolutely requires it of you.

Resolution

When a Decider vote yields a small minority of dissenters, the proposer quickly leads the team, in a highly structured fashion, to deal with them. The Resolution protocol promotes forward momentum by focusing on bringing dissenters in at least cost.

Steps

1. Proposer asks each dissenter "What will it take to get you in?"

2. Dissenter states in a single, short, declarative sentence the precise modification he or she requires to be in.

3. Proposer offers to adopt the dissenter's changes or withdraws the proposal.

Notes

- If the dissenter's changes are simple, the proposer performs a simple eye check to determine if everyone is still in.

- If the dissenter's changes are complex, the proposer must withdraw the current proposal and then submit a new proposal that incorporates the dissenter's changes.

- If the dissenter begins to explain why he or she voted no or anything other than what it will take to get him or her in, the proposer must interrupt the outlier with "What will it take to get you in?"

Perfection Game

The Perfection Game protocol will support you in your desire to aggregate the best ideas. Use it whenever you desire to improve something you've created.

Steps

1. Perfectee performs an act or presents an object for perfection, optionally saying "begin" and "end" to notify the perfector of the start and end of the performance.

2. Perfector rates the value of the performance or object on a scale of 1 to 10 based on how much value the perfector believes he or she can add.

3. Perfector says "What I liked about the performance or object was X," and proceeds to list the qualities of the object the perfector thought were valuable or should be amplified.

4. Perfector offers the improvements to the performance or object required for it to be rated a 10 by saying "To make it a 10, you would have to do X."

Commitments

*   Accept perfecting without argument.

*   Give only positive comments: what you like and what it would take for you to give it a 10.

*   Abstain from mentioning what you don't like or being negative in other ways.

*   Withhold rating points only if you can think of improvements.

*   Use ratings that reflect a scale of improvement rather than a scale of how much you liked the object.

*   If you cannot say something you liked about the object or specifically say how to make the object better, you must give it a 10.

Notes

- A rating of 10 means you are unable to add value, and a rating of 5 means you will specifically describe how to make the object at least twice as good.

- The important information to transmit in the Perfection Game protocol improves the performance or object. For example, "The ideal sound of a finger snap for me is one that is crisp, has sufficient volume, and startles me somewhat. To get a 10, you would have to increase your crispness."

- Perfectee may only ask questions to clarify or gather more information for improvement. If you disagree with the ideas given to you, simply don't include them.

Personal Alignment

The Personal Alignment protocol helps you penetrate deeply into your desires and find what's blocking you from getting what you want. Use it to discover, articulate, and achieve what you want. The quality of your alignment will be equal to the quality of your results.

Steps

1. Want: Answer the question, "What specifically do I want?"

2. Block: Ask yourself, "What is blocking me from having what I want?"

3. Virtue: Figure out what would remove this block by asking yourself, "What virtue, if I had it, would shatter this block of mine?"

4. Shift: Pretend the virtue you identified is actually what you want.

5. Again: Repeat steps 2 to 4 until this process consistently yields a virtue that is powerful enough to shatter your blocks and get you what you originally thought you wanted.

6. Done: Now write down a personal alignment statement in the form, "I want [virtue]." For example, "I want courage."

7. Signal/Response/Assignment: Create a signal to let others know when you are practicing your alignment, and provide a response they can give you to demonstrate support. For example, "When I say/do 'X,' will you say/do 'Y'?" Optionally, turn it into an assignment by saying you will do X a certain number of times per day, where X equals an activity that requires you to practice living your alignment.

8. Evidence: Write, in specific and measurable terms, the long-term evidence of practicing this alignment.

9. Help: Ask each member of your group for help. They help by giving the response you would like when you give your signal that you are practicing your alignment.

Commitments

- Identify an alignment that will result in your personal change and require no change from any other person.

- Identify blocks and wants that are specific and personal.

- Identify blocks that, if solved, would radically increase your effectiveness in life, work, and play.

- Choose a virtue that is about you and preferably one word long. For example: integrity, passion, self-care, peace, fun.

- Ask for help from people who know you and/or know the alignments.

- Identify evidence that is measurable by an objective third party.

Notes

- The most popular personal alignments are "I want (integrity, courage, passion, peace, self-awareness or self-care)."

- If you are struggling with figuring out what you want, adopt the alignment, "I want self-awareness." There is no case where increased self-awareness would not be beneficial.

- A personal block is something you find within yourself. It does not refer to circumstances or other people. Assume that you could have had what you want by now, that your block is a myth that somehow deprives you of your full potential.

- Ideally, identify both immediate and long-term evidence of your alignment. Write down results that start now (or very soon), as well as results you'll see at least five or more years in the future.

- As a default signal, tell your teammates or others who are close to you that you are working on your alignment when you are practicing it. If they don't know the protocol, just tell them what virtue you are working on and ask for their help.

- When members of a team are completing their personal alignments together (asking each other for help), the final step of the process is most powerful if done as a ceremony.

Investigate

The Investigate protocol allows you to learn about a phenomenon that occurs in someone else. Use it when an idea or behavior someone is presenting seems poor, confusing, or simply interesting.

Steps

1. Act as if you were a detached but fascinated inquirer, asking questions until your curiosity is satisfied or you no longer want to ask questions.

Commitments

• Ask well-formed questions.

• Ask only questions that will increase your understanding.

• Ask questions only if the subject is engaged and appears ready to answer more.

• Refrain from offering opinions.

• Do not ask leading questions when you think you know how your subject will answer.

• If you cannot remain a detached, curious investigator with no agenda, stop using the protocol until you can come back to it and keep these commitments.

Notes

• Do not theorize about the subject or provide any sort of diagnosis.

• Consider using the following forms for your questions:

  - What about X makes you Y, Z?

  - Would you explain a specific example?

  - How does X go when it happens?

  - What is the one thing you want most from solving X?

  - What is the biggest problem you see regarding X now?

  - What is the most important thing you could do right now to help you with X?

- Ineffective queries include questions that:
  - lead or reflect an agenda,
  - attempt to hide an answer you believe is true,
  - invite stories, or
  - begin with "why".
- Stick to your intention of gathering more information.
- If you feel that you will explode if you can't say what's on your mind, you shouldn't speak at all. Consider checking your intention or checking out.